PETS ROCK™

MORE FUN THAN FAME

PETS ROCK™

MORE FUN THAN FAME

teNeues

FOR THE LOVE OF PETS

If a Martian landed on earth, was taken to a bunker, and given only an iPhone with a browser and a few apps—Instagram, Twitter, Tumblr—it might come to the very logical conclusion, after just a few scrolls, that pets rule this world.

Let's be real—there are only two things us *homo sapiens* universally know how to worship: pets and celebrities. Endlessly compelling, exuding envy-inducing international appeal, sagely reticent in interviews (all the better for avoiding scandal and controversy!), and—perhaps most importantly—innately adept at starring in viral content, animals are the OG lifestyle influencers. They handle paparazzi with an elegant nonchalance, and are effortlessly iconic and timeless in their demeanor. The more than ten million humans who tune in each year for the *Puppy Bowl* know what's up.

And that's before you even put some clothes on them.

Sure, your dog has never starred in a movie or run an orphanage, and your cat definitely did not come up with the theory of relativity—but hey, no reality show contestant or YouTuber has either. We think we own the pets, but we are, in fact, owned by the pets. We're the stans to their irresistible appeal. Because pets are just so ridiculously cool; they are all "It girls" and (good) boys that inspire our devotion—even if many of them act as if they could not care less about us.

(Kitties, we're looking at you.) What makes them so irresistibly, compulsively popular is their air of otherworldliness.

In other words: Pets rock because they are just living their best lives.

AUS LIEBE ZU UNSEREN VIERBEINERN

Angenommen, ein Außerirdischer landet auf der Erde, wird in einen Bunker gebracht und verfügt dort nur über ein iPhone mit einem Browser und ein paar Apps – Instagram, Twitter, Tumblr –, dann würde dieser nach einigen Scrolls höchstwahrscheinlich zu dem logischen Schluss kommen, dass Vierbeiner die Welt regieren.

Aber nun zurück zur Realität. Es gibt nur zwei Dinge, die der *Homo Sapiens* im Allgemeinen anbetet: Haustiere und Promis. Die einfach faszinierenden Vierbeiner, die mit ihrer internationalen Anziehungskraft jeden Promi vor Neid erblassen lassen, sich in Interviews in weiser Zurückhaltung üben (der beste Weg, um Skandale und Kontroversen zu vermeiden!) und – was vielleicht am wichtigsten ist – über eine angeborene Begabung zum Internet-Star verfügen, sind die wahren Lifestyle-Influencer. Paparazzi begegnen sie mit eleganter Lässigkeit, sie sind unangestrengt charismatisch und legen stets einen tadellosen Auftritt hin. Die mehr als zehn Millionen Menschen, die jedes Jahr den *Puppy Bowl* verfolgen, wissen, was Sache ist.

Und wartet ab, was erst los ist, wenn sie angezogen sind.

Klar, dein Hund hat nie die Hauptrolle in einem Film gespielt oder ein Waisenhaus geleitet, und deine Katze nicht die Relativitätstheorie erfunden – aber hey, das kann auch kein Reality-Show-Teilnehmer oder YouTuber von sich behaupten.

Wir denken, dass Haustiere uns gehören, aber in Wirklichkeit *gehören wir* den Haustieren. Wir verfallen ihrem unwiderstehlichen Charme. Denn die Vierbeiner sind einfach unglaublich *cool*; sie sind alle „It-Girls und -Boys", denen wir völlig ergeben sind – auch wenn sie selbst oft den Eindruck erwecken, als seien wir ihnen völlig egal (ja, liebe Kätzchen, ihr seid gemeint). Was sie so unwiderstehlich macht, ist ihr schräger, etwas surrealer Charakter.

Mit anderen Worten: Die niedlichen Tierchen „rocken", weil sie das Leben voll auskosten.

POUR L'AMOUR DES ANIMAUX DE COMPAGNIE

Si un Martien débarquait sur terre, était emmené dans un bunker, et ne recevait qu'un iPhone avec un navigateur et quelques applications – Instagram, Twitter, Tumblr – il pourrait, après quelques recherches, arriver à la conclusion très logique que les animaux de compagnie dirigent ce monde.

Soyons réalistes – il n'y a que deux choses que nous, les *homo sapiens*, savons universellement vénérer : les animaux de compagnie et les célébrités. Sans cesse convaincants, suscitant l'envie et l'attrait international, sagement réticents dans les interviews (ce qui est le meilleur moyen d'éviter le scandale et la controverse !), et – peut-être plus important encore – naturellement habiles à jouer les vedettes dans le contenu viral, les animaux sont les influenceurs du style de vie des Original Gangsters. Ils manipulent les paparazzi avec une élégante nonchalance, et sont sans effort iconiques et intemporels dans leur comportement. Les plus de dix millions d'humains qui regardent le *Puppy Bowl* chaque année savent de quoi il retourne.

Et tout cela avant même que vous ne les habilliez de vêtements.

Bien sûr, votre chien n'a jamais joué dans un film ou dirigé un orphelinat, et votre chat n'a certainement pas inventé la théorie de la relativité – mais bon, aucun participant à une émission de télé-réalité ou YouTuber non plus. Nous pensons que nous possédons les animaux de compagnie, mais en fait, nous sommes *possédés* par les animaux de compagnie. Nous tombons sous leur charme irrésistible. Parce que les animaux de compagnie sont si incroyablement *cool* ; ce sont toutes des « It girls » et des (bons) garçons qui inspirent notre dévotion – même si beaucoup d'entre eux agissent comme s'se moquaient complètement de nous. (Chatons, c'est vous qu'on vous regarde.) Ce qui les rend si irrésistiblement et compulsivement populaires, c'est leur air de venir d'ailleurs.

En d'autres termes : Les animaux domestiques sont cool parce qu'ils vivent une meilleure vie.

HISTORY, ROYALS & RELIGION

The love of pets is as old as time, and pets are the crown jewels of their owners' lives. We name, feed, care for, and devote endless hours to thinking of them—they are the devotional, omnipotent, and noble sovereigns that reign over us mere, mere mortals.

Given that we revere pets as much (or more) than we revere our human leaders and gurus, it seems appropriate that they could don the regalia of the highest order, that they announce themselves in the suits, gowns, robes, habits, and distinguished military uniforms associated with the utmost power and influence. A bulldog seems as fitting as any leader to march us into war, and who is to say a guinea pig wouldn't do better as president of the United States. All hail the mighty pet, and God save the feline!

GESCHICHTE, ROYALS & RELIGION

Die Liebe zu Haustieren ist so alt wie die Welt, und die süßen Tierchen sind der Lebensmittelpunkt ihrer Herrchen und Frauchen. Wir geben ihnen Namen, füttern und pflegen sie und verbringen unzählige Stunden damit, an sie zu denken – sie sind allmächtige und erhabene Herrscher, die uns gemeine Sterbliche regieren.

Da wir unsere Haustiere genauso sehr verehren wie unsere menschlichen Anführer und Gurus (wenn nicht sogar mehr), erscheint es nur angemessen, dass sie die höchsten Insignien der Macht tragen und sich in den Umhängen, Roben, Ornaten und militärischen Uniformen präsentieren, die mit Macht und Einfluss in Verbindung gebracht werden. Gibt es einen würdigeren Anführer als eine Bulldogge, um die Truppen in den Krieg zu führen und wer behauptet, dass ein Meerschweinchen seine Sache nicht besser machen würde als der Präsident der Vereinigten Staaten? Gegrüßt seist du, mächtiger Vierbeiner, und Gott segne die Katzen!

HISTOIRE, ROYAUMES ET RELIGION

L'amour des animaux de compagnie est aussi vieux que le temps, et ceux-ci sont les joyaux de la couronne de la vie de leurs propriétaires. Nous les nommons, les nourrissons, les soignons et consacrons des heures interminables à penser à eux – ils sont les souverains objets de dévotion, omnipotents et nobles qui règnent sur nous, simples, simples mortels.

Étant donné que nous vénérons les animaux de compagnie autant (ou plus) que nos leaders et gourous humains, il semble approprié qu'ils puissent revêtir les atours de l'ordre le plus élevé, qu'ils se présentent dans les costumes, les robes, les habits, et les uniformes militaires distingués associés aux plus grandes puissance et influence. Un bulldog semble aussi apte que n'importe quel leader à nous faire entrer en guerre, et qui dit qu'un cochon de Guinée ne ferait pas mieux comme président des États-Unis... Saluez tous le puissant animal de compagnie, et que Dieu sauve le félin !

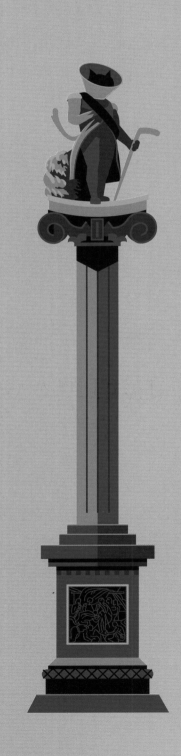

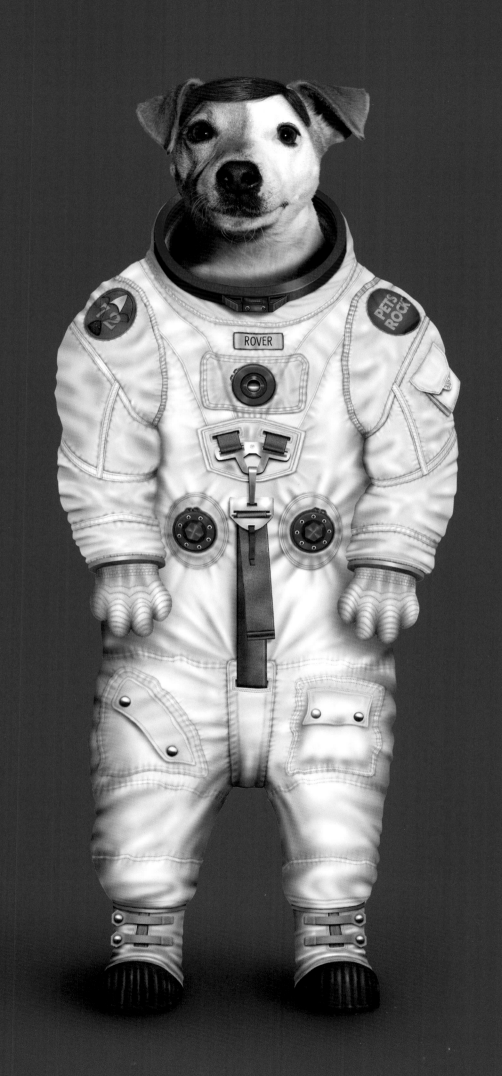

ART, LITERATURE & FASHION

From an aloof feline tastemaker in a severe bob (who slays with her withering "Do you think I'm impressed?" gaze down the whiskers) to the scruffy-looking pop-culture genius who is *definitely* gonna get more than his fifteen minutes of fame, pets are effortless style icons. Who among us would dare to ignore the influencing cue from a feline with a hot (natural) cat eye, or a trendsetting pup (from which species #RBF literally takes its name)?

Lest you think pets can only pull off what is *au courant*—oh no, they can do retro. (Hello, houndstooth.) And we defy you to find a better a model for indigenous Mexican dress than an honest-to-god Chihuahua.

These iconic characters are thoroughly off the leash.

KUNST, LITERATUR & MODE

Vom unnahbaren Trendsetter aus der Familie der Felidae mit seinem strengen Bob (dessen vernichtender Blick über die Schnurrhaare hinweg „Denkst du, du kannst mich beeindrucken?" sagt) bis hin zum Popkultur-Genie im Gammellook, das *garantiert* mehr als fünfzehn Minuten Ruhm ernten wird – Vierbeiner sind geborene Stilikonen. Wer von uns würde es wagen, den Wink einer betörenden Katze mit heißer Cat-Eye-Brille oder eines modebewussten Welpen (das perfekte #RBF) zu ignorieren?

Glaubt aber ja nicht, die pelzigen Tierchen stehen nur auf den letzten Schrei – oh nein, die können auch Retro (Hahnentritt lässt grüßen). Und ihr würdet bestimmt kein besseres Modell für indigene mexikanische Mode finden als einen waschechten Chihuahua.

Diese kultigen Vierbeiner sind absolut umwerfend.

ART, LITTÉRATURE & MODE

Qu'il s'agisse d'un lanceur de mode félin à l'air distant dans un sévère sautillement (qui tue avec son regard cinglant du haut de ses moustaches « Tu crois m'impressionner ?») ou d'un génie de la pop-culture à l'air débraillé qui va *certainement* obtenir plus que ses quinze minutes de gloire, les animaux de compagnie sont des icônes du style sans effort. Qui parmi nous oserait ignorer l'influence d'un félin au bouillant œil de chat (naturel) ou d'un chiot à la mode (#RBF tirant littéralement son nom de son espèce) ?

De peur que vous pensiez que les animaux ne peuvent faire que ce qui est *à la page* – oh non, ils peuvent donner dans le ré-tro. (Bonjour, pied-de-poule.) Et nous vous mettons au défi de trouver un meilleur modèle de robe mexicaine indigène qu'un fervent chihuahua.

Ces personnages emblématiques ne sont pas du tout en laisse.

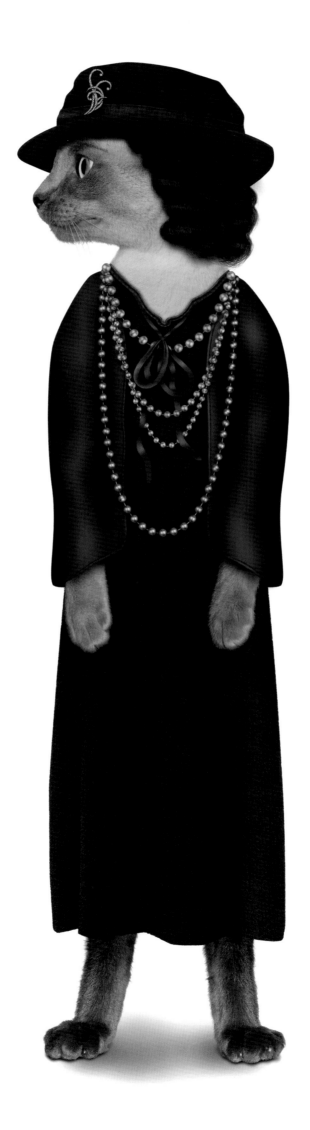

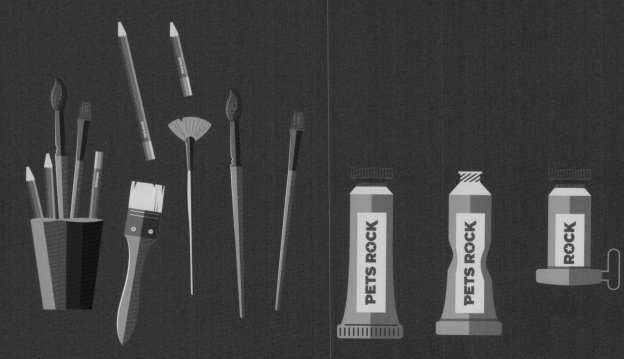

FILM & COMEDY

And now we present perhaps our most illustrious pack of pets, the charismatic, ready-for-their-close-up darlings of the screen: bulldog bombshells, feline femme fatales, heroes of the "tall dog and handsome" variety, and that single kitty who slinks into the kitchen in the morning purring for her *Breakfast*.

Vehemently anti-method acting, these pets don't so much disappear into their roles as they imbue them with unpredictable charm, pathos, and menace. Who wouldn't be freaked out by the dead-on stare of a legit Doberman that clearly expresses, in the international language of animal: "You talking to me?"

We are *definitely* not in Kansas anymore.

FILM & COMEDY

Und nun präsentieren wir unsere wahrscheinlich illustreste Vierbeiner-Gruppe, charismatische Bildschirmlieblinge, die stets für eine Großaufnahme zu haben sind: granatenmäßige Bulldoggen, katzenhafte Femmes fatales, Hundehelden des Varieté und ein Single-Kätzchen, das morgens schnurrend sein *Frühstück* verlangend in die Küche schleicht.

Als vehemente Gegner des Method Acting verstecken sich die Vierbeiner nicht hinter ihrer Rolle, sondern verleihen ihr unerwarteten Charme, Pathos oder gar einen bedrohlichen Charakter. Wem würde der messerscharfe starre Blick eines echten Dobermanns, der einem in der internationalen

Tier-Sprache entgegnet „Redest du mit mir?", keine Gänsehaut einjagen?

Jetzt befinden wir uns *ganz sicher* nicht mehr in Kansas.

CINÉMA & COMÉDIE

Et maintenant, nous vous présentons peut-être notre plus illustre meute d'animaux de compagnie, les charismatiques chouchous de l'écran, prêts pour leur gros plan : les bombes bulldogs, les femmes félines fatales, les héros de la variété « chien grand et beau », et ce chaton célibataire qui se faufile dans la cuisine le matin en ronronnant pour son obtenir *petit déjeuner*.

Jouant avec véhémence à l'encontre de toute méthode, ces animaux de compagnie ne disparaissent pas tant dans leurs rôles car ils leur confèrent un charme, un pathos et une menace imprévisibles. Qui ne serait pas effrayé par le regard fixe d'un doberman sérieux qui exprime clairement, dans le langage animal international : « C'est à moi que vous parlez ?»

Nous ne sommes *très certainement* plus au Kansas.

PETS ROCK™
THE MOVIE

SCENE: | DATE: | LONDON
PRW 1 | 2008 | UK

DIRECTOR

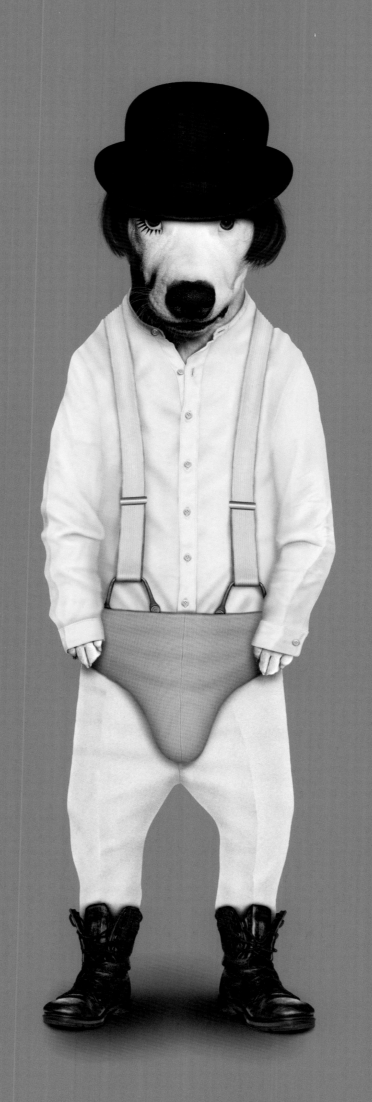

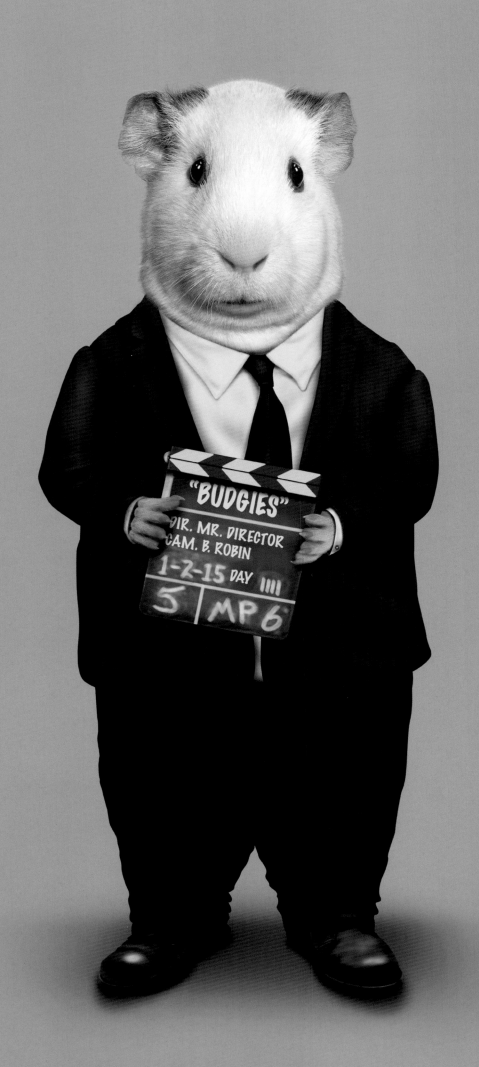

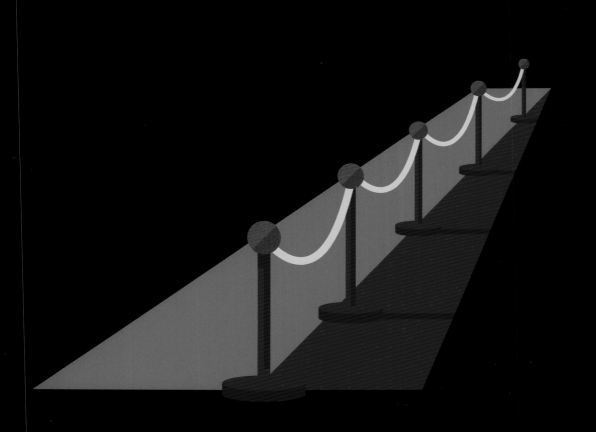

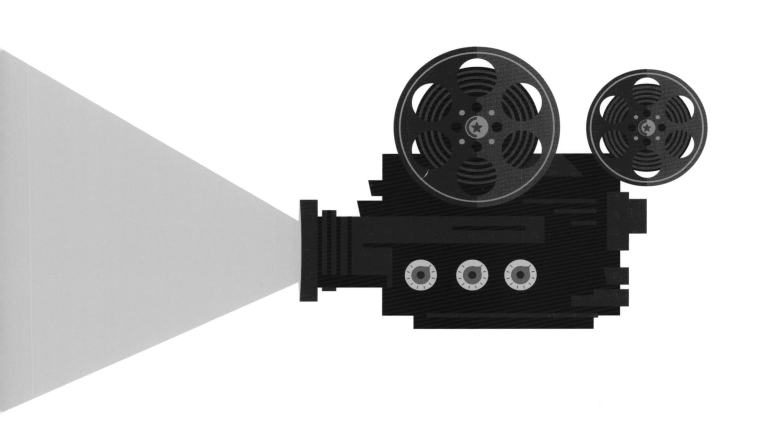

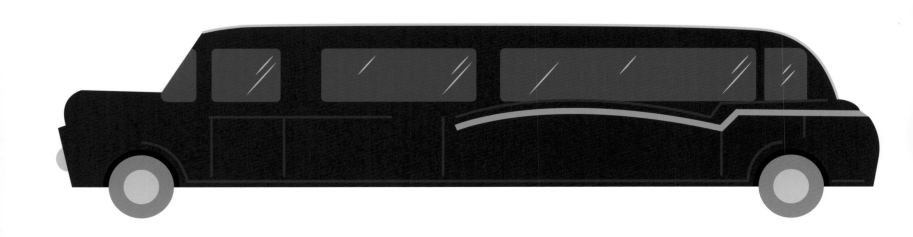

MUSIC

As stars of countless viral videos and TikToks, and instigators of many-a-social-media meme, our pets know how to command an audience. Is kitten twerking a thing? Oh yes, it is a *thing*.

These animal *artistes* are geniuses of pop, and masters of self-reinvention, in any musical genre. Glam hamsters? Check. Hip-hop hounds? Word. Country kitties? You betcha. Divas? Every litter's got at least one. And if you think hair metal is extreme, just check out what these cats can do with their fur.

These party animals clearly have the chops to go the distance, and the star power to light up a stadium. And like all of the GOATs, these pets need only go by a single name.

MUSIK

Als Stars zahlloser viraler Videos und TikToks und Initiatoren unzähliger Social Media-Memes wissen unsere vierbeinigen Freunde genau, wie man ein Publikum fesselt. Twerkt das Kätzchen da etwa? Oh ja, ganz *eindeutig*.

Diese tierischen *Künstler* sind Pop-Genies und Meister der Selbsterfindung, ganz gleich in welchem musikalischen Genre sie zuhause sind. Glamour-Hamster? Check. Hip-hop-Hunde? Kein Problem. Country-Kätzchen? Na klar. Divas? Mindestens eine pro Wurf. Und wenn du glaubst, dass Hair Metal schon extrem ist, dann schau erstmal, was diese Katzen mit Ihrem Fell anstellen.

Diese Partylöwen werden definitiv ihren Weg machen und haben die nötige Star-Power, um ihr Publikum in Ekstase zu versetzen. Und wie bei allen Megastars reicht ihr einziger Name, um ganze Stadien zu füllen.

MUSIQUE

En tant que vedettes d'innombrables vidéos virales et TikToks, et instigateurs de nombreux mèmes de médias sociaux, nos animaux de compagnie savent comment commander un public. Le chaton est en train de faire un twerk, est-ce remarquable ? Oh oui, c'est *remarquable*.

Ces *artistes* animaux sont des génies de la pop, et des maîtres de l'auto-réinvention, et ce dans tous les genres musicaux. Hamsters glam ? Bien sûr ! Chiens de chasse Hip-hop ? Yo ! Chattons country ? Tu parles ! Divas ? Chaque portée en possède au moins une. Et si vous pensez que le glam métal est extrême, regardez ce que ces chats peuvent faire avec leur fourrure.

Ces animaux fêtards ont tout ce qu'il faut pour tenir la distance et le potentiel pour embraser un stade entier. Et comme tous les GOAT, on les appelle par leur petit nom.

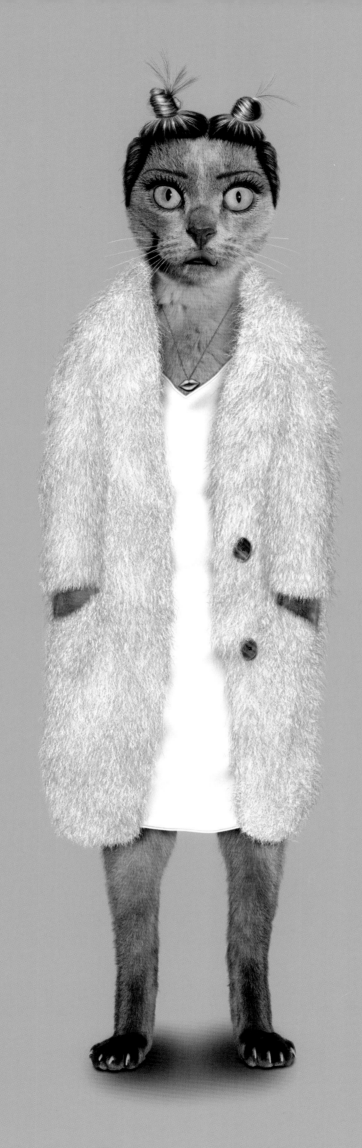

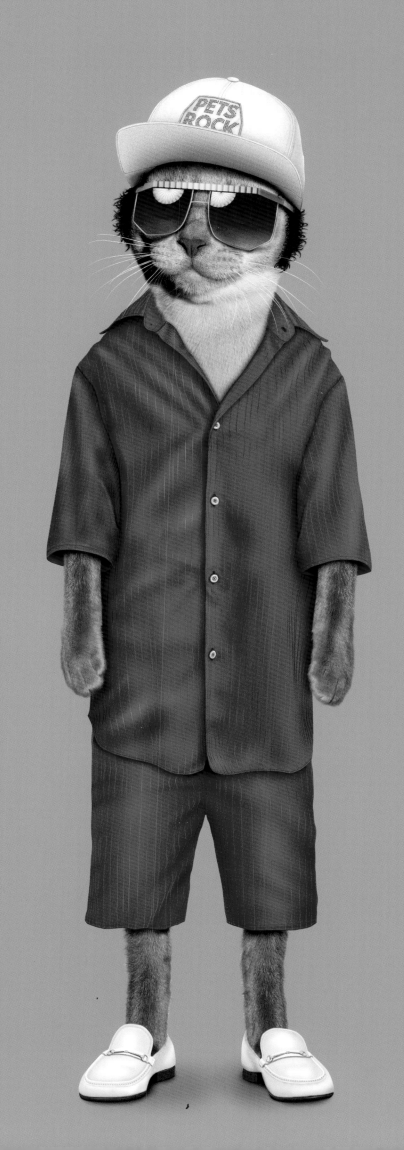

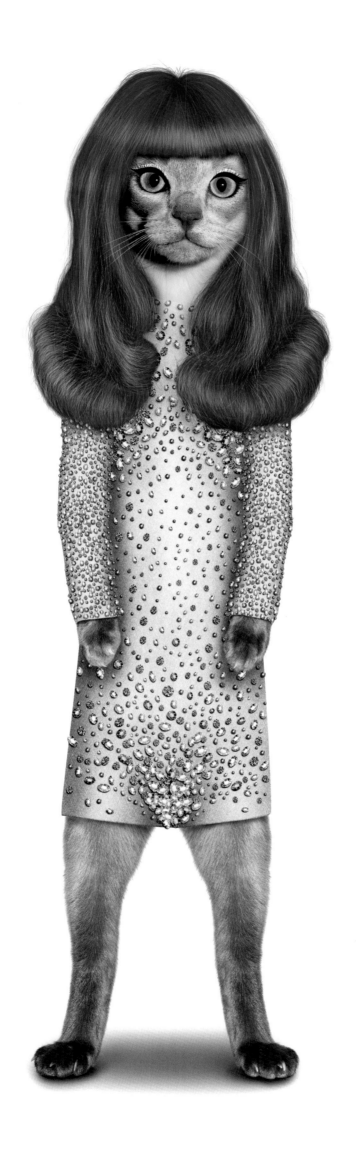

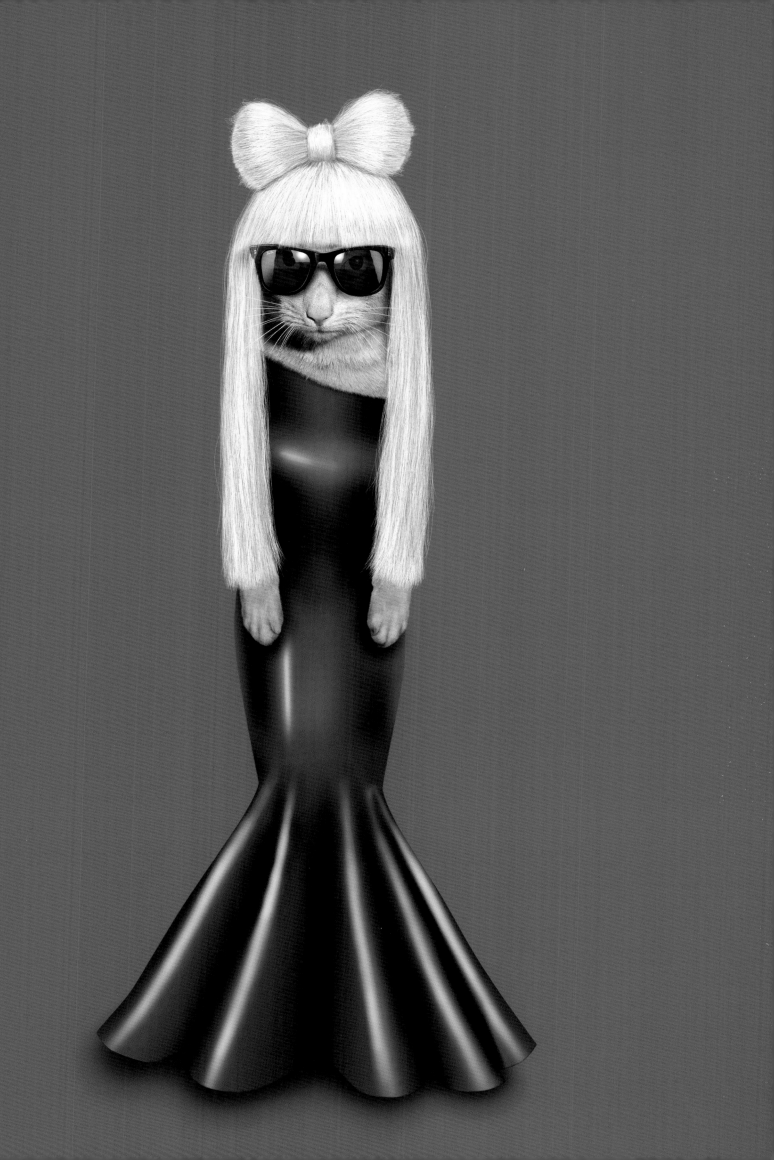

ABOUT PETS ROCK

Launched in 2008, the award winning brand Pets Rock® is a striking play on our enduring fascination with pets and the cult of celebrity. The old adage that 'People look like their pets' led to the creation of characters that brought this saying to life.

Its creators, Mark and Kate Polyblank, are a London based photography and design partnership.

The characters are created by photographing pets, then drawing every other part of the image. That's everything else—hair, clothes, make-up, props. It's all drawn by hand to create a unique work of art.

The Pets Rock® brand is taking its name literally as its unique humour and style spreads around the globe where they have found fans barking mad for these furry friends.

With over 80 characters in the Pets Rock® world and many more waiting to be let off the leash you're never far from one of our pop culture pets.

www.petsrock.co.uk

ÜBER PETS ROCK

Das 2008 erschienene und preisgekrönte Label Pets Rock® spielt effektvoll mit unserer anhaltenden Faszination für Haustiere und dem allgegenwärtigen Promi-Kult. Der alte Spruch „Wie das Frauchen, so das Wauwauchen" liegt der Entstehung der tierischen Protagonisten zugrunde, die diese Redensart zum Leben erwecken.

Ihre Schöpfer, Mark und Kate Polyblank, arbeiten im Bereich Fotografie und Design zusammen.

Die Charaktere entstehen in zwei Etappen: Zuerst werden die Vierbeiner fotografiert und später alle anderen Bestandteile des Bildes zeichnerisch hinzugefügt, z.B. Haare, Kleider, Make-up oder Requisiten. All dies ist handgezeichnet und so entsteht ein einzigartiges Kunstwerk.

Das Label Pets Rock® macht seinem Namen alle Ehre: Der einzigartige Humor und Stil sind ein Riesenerfolg und weltweit sind Fans völlig verrückt nach den knuddeligen Tierchen.

Mit über 80 Charakteren in der Pets Rock®-Welt und noch vielen mehr, die darauf warten, von der Leine gelassen zu werden, sind unsere Popkultur-Vierbeiner praktisch überall anzutreffen.

www.petsrock.co.uk

À PROPOS DE PETS ROCK

Lancée en 2008, la marque primée Pets Rock® est un jeu saisissant concernant notre fascination durable pour les animaux de compagnie et le culte de la célébrité. Le vieil adage selon lequel « les gens ressemblent à leurs animaux de compagnie » a conduit à la création de personnages qui ont donné vie à ce dicton.

Ses créateurs, Mark et Kate Polyblank, forment un partenariat de photographie et de design basé à Londres.

Les personnages sont créés en photographiant des animaux de compagnie, puis en dessinant toutes les autres parties de l'image. C'est tout le reste – cheveux, vêtements, maquillage, accessoires. Tout est dessiné à la main pour créer une œuvre d'art unique.

La marque Pets Rock® prend son nom au pied de la lettre alors que son humour et son style uniques se diffusent partout dans le monde où ils ont trouvé des fans aboyant de folie pour ces amis à fourrure.

Avec plus de 80 personnages dans le monde de Pets Rock® et bien d'autres qui attendent qu'on détache la laisse, vous n'êtes jamais loin d'un de nos animaux de compagnie de la culture pop.

www.petsrock.co.uk

IMPRINT

Texts by Caitlin Leffel
Copyediting by Dr Suzanne Kirkbright,
Artes Translations
Translations by STAR Software, Translation,
Artwork, Recording GmbH

Design by Jens Grundei, teNeues Media
Editorial coordination by
Inga Wortmann-Grützmacher, teNeues Media
Production by Sandra Jansen-Dorn, teNeues Media
Color separation by Jens Grundei, teNeues Media

ISBN 978-3-96171-248-9
Library of Congress Number: 2019956727

Printed in Italy by Lito Terrazzi S.r.l.

FSC
www.fsc.org
MIX
Papier aus verantwor-
tungsvollen Quellen
FSC® C016466

Bibliographic information published by the Deutsche Nationalbibliothek
The Deutsche Nationalbibliothek lists this publication in the Deutsche Nationalbibliografie; detailed bibliographic data are available on the Internet at http://dnb.dnb.de.

Published by teNeues Publishing Group

teNeues Media GmbH & Co. KG
Am Selder 37, 47906 Kempen, Germany
Phone: +49-(0)2152-916-0
Fax: +49-(0)2152-916-111
e-mail: books@teneues.com

Press department: Andrea Rehn
Phone: +49-(0)2152-916-202
e-mail: arehn@teneues.com

teNeues Media GmbH & Co. KG
Munich Office
Pilotystraße 4, 80538 Munich, Germany
Phone: +49-(0)89-904-213-200
e-mail: bkellner@teneues.com

teNeues Media GmbH & Co. KG
Berlin Office
Mommsenstraße 43, 10629 Berlin, Germany
Phone: +49-(0)152-0851-1064
e-mail: ajasper@teneues.com

teNeues Publishing Company
350 7th Avenue, Suite 301, New York, NY 10001, USA
Phone: +1-212-627-9090
Fax: +1-212-627-9511

teNeues Publishing UK Ltd.
12 Ferndene Road, London SE24 0AQ, UK
Phone: +44-(0)20-3542-8997

teNeues France S.A.R.L.
39, rue des Billets, 18250 Henrichemont, France
Phone: +33-(0)2-4826-9348
Fax: +33-(0)1-7072-3482
www.teneues.com

teNeues Publishing Group
Kempen
Berlin
London
Munich
New York
Paris

teNeues